# While Sleeping

## Bill Lavender

Chax Press ❦ Tuscon ❦ 2004

Acknowledgement is gratefully given to *Fell Swoop*, *Exquisite Corpse*, and *5_Trope*, where many of these poems first appeared.

Cover Art: Nancy Dixon and Bill Lavender
Book Design: Bill Lavender

ISBN 0-925904-36-8

CHAX PRESS
101 W. SIXTH STREET
TUCSON, AZ
85701-1000

Poetry and sleep have always been related to me. What do we seek when we lie down to rest but a pleasant landscape of language? inaudible rehearsals of the auditory, invisible practice of the visual. To rehearse the poem that does nothing more than call up relaxed and relaxing frame of the rehearsal, for the poem has always aspired to sleep and sleep to the poem, referent beyond logic and logic beyond referent. It is possible of course to be asleep and awake at the same time, indeed we are mostly, examples: driving the freeway and missing the exit engrossed in meditation, or better the ineluctable state of napping in my chair, when I leave me there and go out for closer observation, hearing even seeing everything that goes on around but not noticing my own snores.

Insomnia being a condition of language, an unsettling complication of a thing that never was a thing to begin with. After all, no one ever thought to accuse prepositions of standing for something– like winos in the park no one's ever going to ask *them* to run for office.

I have brothers, sisters, aunts and uncles too, but all flee on approaching this corpus. One is either with you or against you here, some weird hybrid of equals sign and plus and minus, or like the sigmas inserted among the numbers, tiny insects that suck blood and are resilient. You, that is one, has no relations. The entire edifice depends on these shaky underpinnings that have to be shored up every night, or like an old suzuki taken apart and oiled and cleaned and simply fucked with if there's any hope of it running tomorrow. And lots of times there isn't and machines do recombine with earth again just like bodies and we leave them both behind and get on like a haiku sleeping.

She dreams about me and wakes up mad and that is my fault. The world is this nexus, dreamt of blame, linguistic reparation based on a weave of sleeps that stretch to adam (or whatever that variable may signify). Money talks literally here, mouthing pretense and value and identity at the biggest poetry reading in the universe. Each time we think we've come to the end play continues into sleep, and then begins. Time is a bedouin bivouacked in this purchasing power.

Such visions coalesce in the good intentions of willful thought, the moral imperative that keeps us from being beasts but doesn't stop us from eating them. Succubus on an old greyhound with a wine bottle rolling around the floor at every turn and brake, how could one sleep through that?

Having said that, the poem would seem to demand itself like a pond freezing over. We tend to view them as permanent, which I suppose they relatively are, but not for the reason you'd think, the formulation of time being made in the yin yan of the permanently and putatively real, an estate which will neither sell nor be spoken but simply melt. What betokens the primal and/or final flip of the lever. All we can do is imagine a conflagration that destroys record of the question.

A real circle is imperfect so there aren't any but the dotted line that corrals an identity; you won't find any argument with polyvalence but willing containment in an (real, paginated) arena where concepts vie for their birthright as activities. Strife, as the god said, being the only constant, ease the invented relation that allows us to see sleep as the sea beyond the mountain of awareness, struggle, starvation, working toward that only thing that comes utterly without effort.

New Orleans, October 2003

# While Sleeping

for Nanc

1

Outside the university building
four boys take turns preaching.
One's wearing a tee shirt with
BIBLE stenciled on the back
No one is listening. When I
walk by I try not to look at them
and they try not to look at me.


2

young woman on her way to class
        will go to her grave
having never read a word
        about Plato's cave


3

*jihad*
        the corporate war
*jihad*
        the thinning of humanity
        the clawing to the top
*jihad*
        enron ceo sells stock for 17 million
*jihad*
        the whole world in the hands
of broken men bent on plunder and revenge

4

What ever became
of antibiotic orthodoxy?


5

school loan—
need to remember to reinstate
automatic debit


6

after reading the clark
biography of olson I confess
i'd rather not be alone too
      much—
or all the sea in china.


7

I set off on mental journey
where will I find myself?
Now I've doubled
and in this realization tripled
and in this quadrupled &
      forgot to set the alarm

8

Fedex knocks on the door this evening—
wants to leave a package for someone
named Guzman. I've never heard of
Guzman. My neighbor.

9

They say these patterns
I see when I close my eyes
are common to us all—
this one's breaking up.

10

Poet in the bathtub singing
*Poet in New York*

11

The cat loves most
to rub the corner of her mouth
on the corner of the book
I am reading.
Then she drags her butthole on
    the sheet.

## 12

what i want to ask clark is
yes you wrote this thing and it's lovely
 but do you *believe* it?
  do you *believe* in biography?

## 13

 May the yawn that transcendeth
 all understanding
 be with me now
 & tomorrow evening.

## 14

Words weasel out
 where ontology only surfaces...
  owning vs. belonging

## 15

her breath rectangular part of
the flowing, the snows, something
bestowed not memory but
 residual— trace of the actual

## 16

slept a little this afternoon &
that is impeding

## 17

$$\frac{\text{line virgule line}}{\text{virgule as division}} = \frac{\text{line line}}{\text{as division}}$$

(with "virgule" struck through in both positions on the left side)

## 18

  returning not so much as one any one
returning fall down O with spheres
old sodden nimbus hollering
  OK we're telling everyone now

## 19

My head full of strange aircraft—
then I remember— it's Pearl Harbor Day.

## 20

  on my back
    looking up at trees
clear water washes over me

21

The 2 guys in the desks
in front of me
turn around and look.


22

it's easier to connect the words
than the images like predreams
someone walks by laughing at my
attempt


23

Sunrise, blank, over a form
is it words or *that* I'm after
the shadow of my hand
a noise in the kitchen that isn't the cat


24

an old dream of spirit you'd
think we'd found him out down here
vagaries of linguistic certitude
just getting interesting when I forget to write

## 25

I smell good
I don't care how you sound.


## 26

After you fell asleep
I went over and
stole your pen. *

* Nanc read this & got mad


## 27

I orient to the letters via
    proprioception.
    The way I know what my hand
    is doing behind my back
I understand representations.


## 28

I iron out the kinks in the I


## 29

my eye goes down
i'm face down

## 30

jets flying over—
black on black
then it's midnight
    the noise is a river


## 31

Can poetry matter?
Probably,
   though I'd prefer it didn't.


## 32

ambient drone of the city
    is it a train?
distant sirens
the cat sighs


## 33

An old friend emails in all caps:
THERE ARE PEOPLE OUT THERE WHO,
GIVEN THE OPPORTUNITY, WOULD DO
   US GREAT HARM
and i ask him who is us?

34

Should I revise these poems?
Or revise them before I write them?
Or revise them and say I didn't?


35

After Patricia Hampl
heard me read in Prague
she told me I shd write short stories
but after I heard Patricia Hampl read in Prague
I didn't tell her she shd write poems.


36

Sleep is like fiction—
it draws you in.


37

The wind blew the door open
and I'm blue too.


38

it isn't *me* that's sleeping
you understand

39

something going on outside
that sounds like
    a pack of wolves
bringing down an elk


40

now someone's shoveling
at 12:20 a.m.
that sense of time's
        propriety
  first thing to go


41

maybe out in
the country
things *are*
    getting better


42

```
s k i p
h i l l
i l i a ──────▶ to ma lou
p l a y
```

43

I like it
  when the words
    make scents
     but don't
      like things
       coming too close
     coming
    away happy


44

her grandfather
  peeking out
    from behind the camera & stuff
     up on the dresser


45

when I have grandchildren
  if I do
    everything will be electronic &
    everything will be forgotten

46

noise like a great stomach
rumbling
or a giant piece of furniture sliding
across the floor


47

we're irate
we're innate
we're liberal &
we're too late


48

he'll do anything
say anything, any
sort of lie or insult
or obsequious flattery
to see his tripe in print—
he's the george bush
of the poetry world

49

what does it mean
    to write while sleeping?
   I'm a little fuzzy on it
myself had it
just a moment ago
    & now it's gone


50

motorcycleshift motorcycleshift motorcycle
    that run on the freeway
    this afternoon—
   very scary


51

rap group called
the graveyard soldiers. . .
I'll let them introduce
themselves

### 52

Some friends I love dearly
whose politics I find untenable
and who would find mine radical,
the same sort of thing they might rail about
  over the morning paper—
the micro doesn't jive with the macro—
  they aren't *of* the same thing.

### 53

  3 sleeps:
    writing
    revision
    transcription

### 54

  he has hash
  (she says sash
  we was wash
  they that thrash
  I is ash)

## 55

what is that sound?
it sounds harder than that.

## 56

real people
keep appearing
in these poems
  as if the page were getting cloudy

## 57

the past is trying
to drink me up

## 58

you were lookin at me
just like
everyone
was lookin at me
tonight

## 59

tomorrow is the end of vacation
tomorrow my eyes will be apples

## 60

where the pome
    makes
  an arc
multicolored mumbling mumbo
    jumbo

## 61

terror is the night
  terror error

## 62

I stand up here
  reading this to you
    & only a moment ago
was sleeping

## 63

what occurs to the colors
while they wait
all well and good
and the well is very deep

## 64

the playful nip denotes the bite
but it does not bite
what the note delights

## 65

I hear the floor furnace
expand and contract.
The house expands
and contracts more slowly
and I hear that too.

## 66

of the divorce he sd.
she was a little too crazy
and anyway he
was going to be busy spewing text

## 67

there is nothing outside the text
nor inside either

## 68

I don't dream any more
or else they're
happening while I'm away

## 69

the dog
is a log

## 70

what can I smoke
that'll take me inside
the painting

## 71

whatever—mental or physical—
one might find

72

what just went by &
was so wonderful—
i just missed


73

It's fun
to write elegies.


74

moving toward my eyelids
I come to a cliff edge
horizon receding


76

Do all of you have
that little metapoem
running provisionally
behind everything,
or is it just me?

## 75

I think I am thinking
but can't prove it except
by writing.

## 77

    seamless integration
into
    the semes of intellect
at least
    it seems real enough

## 78

I admire people who
  manage to keep their bitterness intact
  no matter how successful they are.

## 79

  turn out lights
      lock doors
    brush teeth
      set the heat—
thought of 3 or 4
  little poems and forgot them
before i made it to the bed

## 80

you know you're getting old
when you find
you've developed a taste
    for camomille

## 81

Today at the campus
it's freezing and the heat's not working
it's still xmas break and the
parking lots are empty
only a few administrators  like me
hanging around—
still the rumors are flying.

## 82

Thought is a
metaphor
for the private rehearsal
of social activity—
like the cat running
around crazy, ending up
halfway up a tree
though nothing is after her.

83

the politics of writing
has almost nothing to do
with what you say


84

ethics of being—
to have identity
is to have an ethos


85

so long sleep
bleat & reap
small streets weep
for feet that beat them &
heat sweeps the fleet asleep
then speak sweet sleep

86

me thud
  to his hoarseness
out<sup>and then swing third knuckle and was</sup> out


87

must stop petting the cat to write—
she doesn't like it


88

What's it like to get old?
I used to abhor routine;
now I treasure it.


89

that is almost a lie


90

a scarecrow that lasted
through the entire movie

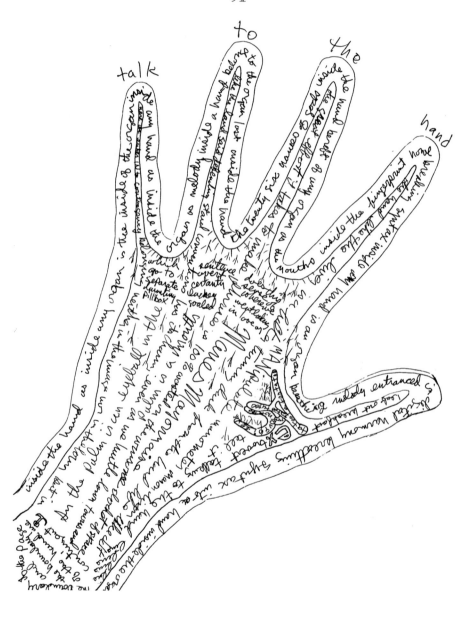

only microscopically
cd. he prove
he loved her
"look in here if you don't
believe me"

too much language period

(*for gina*)


I'm writing this quickly & unpremeditatedly
not only that
 i'm writing it blithely & queroulously & insouciantly
and now i'm getting into it
i'm writing it unpardonably & airily & frivolously & freely
   & cunningly & wastefully & causelessly
& now it's winding down &
i'm writing it motionlessly & rotely & breathlessly &
   copiously & artificially & unacceptably & dentally &
   gentlemanlyly & suspendedly & cornily & homily &
   utterly
without knowing

## 95

*(for bill)*

    family never believed in santa claus
i always thought we'd get
    better presents
if we did


## 96

    No matter how infallible
       your logic
I still feel
          like I'm getting fucked


## 97

    now I begin to understand
      the rightness of it
had I felt this surge
    in my youth
I could not have born it
30 seconds pays for
    a lifetime of drudgery


## 98

the narrative of pretending

99

(she pretending he pretending she
     pretending
  they pretending pretending
pretending he pretending she
     pretending we
  pretending pretending)


100

  outside every nickel
  is a plan
            :repeat


101

    milk the cow
    (build the cow
    filch the cow
    steal a car)


102

  having trouble hearing
  the radio
    all that falling
      around my ears

## 103

the ideal viewing distance:
  how far is it
from my face to the photograph?

## 104

        only a pun
    detritus of meaning
        stages our progress

## 105

The problem with irony is
  it's never quite
    ironic enough—
      the game always verges on
        truth.

## 106

  a
  barrier full of snakes

107

the voices
are vowels
in the towers
of tours


108
*(for )ohn)*

am I paranoid
or does everyone really love me   ?


109

I'm afraid yes I stare
a little too intently
at my computer sometimes.


110

insomnia: a horrible place
cut off from poetry
glad i'm not there

### 111

when the hare's hair's dyed
he died
(deed to the city)

### 112

w-halla-semio-synthesis
pairs of ligh  t
inception
& the crows lay down
in the street

### 113

being it's
own reward
(we'll wheel)

### 114

It isn't racism or sexism or masochism or classism
that needs to be undone—
they'll only replace each other—
but the entire architecture of identity.

## 115

What's the point
    of all this?

The point is a nib
    a indicator
        the point is a geiger counter
            the oint is avuncular
like a pike up yr ass
    coming out yr mouth

## 116

Why feel so alone
facing death?
We do it en masse.

## 117

the words
haven't been themselves
tonight

## 118

I'm Jody Wallace
I'm Bree Matthews

119

a deer's face
　in the wood grain


120

sleep
　the architecture
　of things that tumble down
the scaffolding
　that lets all fall


121

Lucy & Ricky
　matching pajamas.


122

reading these poems
　to my mother
　　she sd. she closed her eyes
& tried to die

## 123

We did not meet
across a bridge of poetry still
    it made me feel I had
something to do.

## 124

*(another triptych: trip to arkansas)*

### I (UP)

a camper shell
  for sale on the roadside
    in Transylvania—
we'll check it out on the way back
    when not in such a hurry

### II (THERE)

How can I help you? <sup>I don't know.</sup>
What do you need? <sup>I don't know.</sup>
What do you want? <sup>I don't know.</sup>
Where do you hurt? <sup>I don't know.</sup>
Do you want a pain pill? <sup>No.</sup>

### III (BACK)

my name's yolanda
i live in yucatan
i sell yucca

The camper's 2 feet
longer than my bed.

## 125

My friends say
I write poems
only my friends can appreciate.
                (was it a friend who sd:
                    "get new friends"?)


## 126

What is a carreer?
I'm not sure
but everyone I know
    who has one
is an asshole.


## 127

one good thing about poetry is
it'll never be collected
            by Andrew Fastow*

* Fastow, financial wizard and
  former CFO of Enron, owns
  one of the largest private
  collections of contemporary
  art in Texas.

## 128

if if was a skiff
we'd be sailin

## 129

The ocean
doesn't mean to be listend to
especially
on the beach in mid winter
like an old movie
seen with new eyes
or starting to smoke
again
at 50

## 130

VIAGRA™ commercial #1:
race car driver
VIAGRA™ commercial #2:
Andrei Codrescu

## 131

new drink:
TV on the beach

## 132

like in the ocean
sound travels more slowly
but much farther
than light

## 133

every silly poet
    and their dog
barks about sound

## 134

Tony Curtis in *The Boston Strangler*
when he sees himself
in the mirror.

## 135

that woman with a stick
    is a guy

## 136

5–10–15–
16 sand dollars
or 981-7673 for dolphin rides

## 137

There's only one word for this
and that word is impactful.

## 138

i'm hooked
on a drug
that doesn't yet exist

## 139

There is a quantifiable mechanics
to aesthetics (social ideological whatever)
    but these quantities are
    (necessarily)
not apprehendible by
  the current language system. . .
    (that's why they call it aesthetics.)

## 140

Paul Newman in *Harper:*
predatory go-go dance—
meaningless trek
through the pop-cultural
labyrinth
honey the market for
happiness
just dried up.

## 141

these poems
so many ways of saying the same
what comes but doesn't
come to mind

## 142

a project that adheres to a certain theme
audience
time frame
publication
form
performance
je ne sais quoi
all of the above
none of the above

## 143

how the pen
can be a sin
or a double agent

## 144

bodies mummified
around the crematorium
it happend
because of inadequate
administrative oversight

## 145

In the long haul
all governments are democratic
rule by consent
even insistence
of the governed.  All we want
out of our slavery:
to be important enough
to be spied upon.

## 146

I spy
U speed
caught on
radar


## 147

drifting off        like momma
    wants
            to drift off
why do they call it nerves?
        what a drag
    to open eyes again


## 148

join the struggle against the police state
join the struggle against the terror
or against corporate rule
or join the struggle against daytime road construction
or against long lines at Wal-Mart
or bad movies in great theatres
    or cheap building construction
    or Japanese cars
or don't join a fucking thing still
    struggle you will

149

If we didn't have the word "play"
how wd. we describe
what the cat is doing?


150

Mildred Lavender
Health House
Emerald City, #115
Fayetteville, AR  72703


151

some big guy
rattling a piece of tin
flashing a strobe
but real snow begins to fall


152

tomorrow i drive in it
to the emerald city

## 153

snow rain hail love hate
  how come everything
that falls from the sky
  has four letters?

## 154

a future configuration
  of the continental plates
  mapped on the ceiling
in water stain

## 155

on the table is a
  BIG BUTTON JAR
and I can't sleep

## 156

Friends we have
of genuine affect
come and go
but political relationships
  are eternal.

## 157

2 states
2 candy bars
& <sup>maybe</sup> a planet

## 158

when it rains
   i worry that the roof will leak
when the sun shines
   i worry that the roof will leak

## 159

The Emerald City provides:
- Health South's® caring, professionally trained, and plentiful staff.
- Clean, pleasant, convenient location.
- All the latest equipment to provide the best of care for you or your loved one.

## 160

Please direct further correspondence
relative to this matter to
anyone but me,
Respectfully submitted,
Signed,
Yours very
truly.

## 163

*(essay on slugs)*

slug-a-bed
salting slugs
slug it out
slug-fest
slug of the earth
sluggo

## 162

some noisy birds down here
the jay
the chirrup
the twitter
caw
& squawk

161

and on the 8th day
god made
sleeping in the rain


164

not knowing where
the language
leaves us
wanting more


165

and the numbers
come alive


166

—broadband calico—
cat for the electronic age

# 167

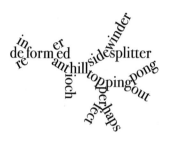

# 168

I fell in the snow &
"bruised a rib"—
one day the pain was in my side,
one day in my chest,
one day in my back,
& one day it migrated all the way
   into my shoulder—something
Wittgenstein might have experienced
   had he lived
        a little longer.

## 169

My "friend"
only plays ping-pong
on a hill, and only him
on top—

dog has pups
now the whole family's
on the roof


## 170

have you seen the new Buick?
the Hearsay.
  it's stateoftheart.


## 171

Somehow I got it in my head
that thoughts exist
in a physical place—a room
where you could go and
    rearrange them
    like furniture.

in
de form ed
re
er
antioch
hill
sidewinder
splitter
topping
pingpong
out
perhaps
perfect

175

the way you feel
    after smoking pot
is the way you should have felt
in the first place

### 176

I scream
you scream
we all scream
in a dream

### 177

imagine each of these poems
is a book—
one hundred seventy seven
books—
an entire city paved with
books

### 178

Instead of fingerprints
these days
we have egg-nog.

### 179

outside the wind is blowing
a new weather moving in
like a flock of blackbirds
in a bamboo stand

## 180

MK loves her some dick—
she forwards email pictures
to all her friends— a sleeping
dick stands up and sings a song—
a dick squeezed between two balls
  to make a dick-burger.

## 181

the old
  "I knew I was gonna get hurt
  so I started hurting early."
defense mechanism

## 182

  me & my
  headstong self

## 183

bare wire sticking out the wall
  what's on the other end?
  not sure but i thinking
      maybe
    the emerald city

## 184

Those who wd. argue for accessibility
in poetry don't realize TV
is the most esoteric of media—
who could understand it without
years of devoted study
of advertising technique,
sitcom formulae, and news codes?

## 185

I think about certain things
that relax me and let me sleep
and try to avoid those thoughts
that upset me and keep me awake.
If we didn't have the word thinking
how wd. we describe what I'm doing?

## 186

the 4 blades of the ceiling fan
form a plane—
the pull-chain that hangs from it
a line perpindicular to that plane—
my body below it
a plane perpindicular to that line.

## 187

my baby
laughs at me
   when I lay down to sleep
   with the notebook on my
     chest

## 188

I'm sleepin with blue fruit—
Nebraska sunset—
    purple and green
  is what I'm seeing—
  maybe a fence.

## 189

I think they charged us
for 2 bottles of wine
at the restaurant tonight,
and we only had one.

## 190

Do you know how hard it is
to type teh adn nto in
Microsoft Word?

191

my my how the nights rush by
even this one
when my sweet angel
left the emerald city
entered the emerald city–


192

*(for Sarah, Janna, and Karl)*

alone in the old house
your ghosts brushed past me in the hall
just knowing
you spent your childhood here
makes the place seem sacred


193

the coffin often
seems to soften
in the ground–
the concrete vault
is for the rest of us

194

why must we
trivialize everything
by writing about it?


195

Suppose I replace myself
  w/ a machine that
every day, twice a day at roughly
the same times
  took a handful of catfood
from the cabinet under the sink
    & put it in her bowl—
wd. she wail incessantly
to make the robot hurry?
      rub on its leg?


196

Dave always has
  a poem or two
    written on the back of his hand

197

all our problems
that seem so irremedial
pass away
            unsolved
and in their place
    new problems
        also irremedial
& this is even true
    in ~~Palestine~~
        radise


198

putting out to sleep
    ran aground
    against this notebook
and
    began to break up


199

metaphors
    how
        tediuos

### 200

when i close my eyes
i see
neon kidney bean (NKB)

### 201

(aside) I can't tell
my lines
from the stage directions

### 202

the grocery store
at 11 PM
isn't just the *American* dream
*jihad*
losing steam
(need for universal
health insurance)

### 203

I look a long time
at the picture on the wall—
an excavation.

204

at the workshop with camille and leslie
    i told a story about my memoir
and in this memoir i as we all do
    shifted a fact or 2 here and there
        to make a more pleasing narrative
then on a trip home i'd driven by one
    of the old haunts and was surprised
        to discover it wasn't as i'd written–
the memoir becomes the memory–
    get it?


205

    there never were any facts
        to begin with


206

    sometimes the cat
        hides her face in her paws
            as if weeping
    or as if she doesn't want to see

## 207

There is no honesty—
   only an honest rage—
   or piety.

## 208

there is-no's
   just as bad
as what-is's

## 209

We americans don't know
how to care for ourselves con
ditiond as we are
to loathe the public space.

## 210

writing by candle light
   writing
by monitor light   either way
   it's a mess

### 211

simul*taneous*titude    transaction
*cast*—this poem & a    (like like)
softball game

### 212

during the 3rd game of the evening
the ump wdn't call
a strike
if his momma was pitching

### 213

not where
words abound
not yet coming
not yet town

### 214

various shades of purple
rivulets
in the candlemelt

215

GETTING
READY
FOR BED
UNDERLINE
HAND
NEVER A
SLACK MOM
ENT IN CY
BERSPACE
BUT IN THE
WEAVE BEY
OND-BAND
WATER SN
AKES DONT
SWIM THEY
JUST GO
WHAT DOES
THE CROWD
MAKE OF
ITS OWN ITS
SOCIAL SP
ACE WHAT
DOES THE WA
TCH FACE SAY

INDIGLO

FRI 4-19
10:0B 38

NOT WHERE
WORDS ABO
UND NOT
YET COMI
NG NOT Y
ET TOWN
DIGITAL
WATCH BAND
LED
POLITICI
ANS TO EN
HANCE TH
E CHAIN
OF REASO
NS AS IF
TAX LAW RAY
WERE CHI
LD'S PLAY
THIS IS R
ATHER LIK
E ONE OF
RANDY'S
POEMS (W
ERE THERE
BUT WORLD
ENOUGH)
+ DAVE A
LWAYS HAS
A POEM OR
TWO WRITT
EN ON THE
BACK OF
HIS HAND

216

the male critique
vs.
critique of the male –
poems of the general genre
(salute)


217

portions of the preceding
are copyright ©
2002 by nancy dixon


218

There is no way to speak of time
without using spatial metaphors
there is no "way"
to speak of anyting
without metaphors of
proximity &
distance.

219

writing these
poems is
        sleeping
in a different bed
every night


220

like Wittgenstein's solipsist
the implied competitor
of our arguments
is usually already dead


221

the time is three sticks
(doubled)


222

a room with a view
(swimming
        pool Q's)

223

shitty as it was
i wish i could
    drive through the snow again
    to the emerald city


224

    as I write in
        this notebook
        bookmarks fall out
& the bookmarks
    are poems
too


225

    the preaching
        doesn't reach
and the writing
        doesn't right
            anything

226

a boy's
fascination
w/
serpents


227

a wire-haired
barrier


229

BANANia
exquis déjeuner
sucré
a la farinae de banane  $$$

how I wish I had some!


228

everynight this struggle
everynight
barely making it
back to sleep

## 230

a new method —
remain standing
until collapse —
this avoids several pitfalls

## 231

cd. there be thought
behind thought
that isn't in the language game?
wd. it be there if
never mentioned?

## 232

shortstop gave me a tump
(on the bike[suzuki])
then

BINK!

unknown portugal

233

does it violate
copyright law
if the asteroid™ Gunship
is present at my
motorcycle wreck?


234

who u think
u are is a year
1995%


235

the following have expired
during creation of this poem:
    momma
    motorcycles
    mike's mother
    mattel co-founder Ruth Handler, survived by & inventor of Barbie and Ken
    meaning
    mazy motion
    music
    mideast peace

236

got fever
these wounds
            suck so hard
need my medicine
                man


237

walnuts
stain everything black
                the old playground
        dissolving in the ink


238

she thought she left
        the book @ the manicurist
        Hover .
what does it mean
        to find something
    when the pen teethes it's
already almost ending

239

this + is at
that

is at

the end of thin

where we begin

&

240

though i shd be
off the pain pills by
now i'm still taking them
cat senses disparity & makes
slight alterations to her routine
sleep comes only after effort
like a trek across wasteland

241

it takes a certain
eloquence
to recall the past
abra
cadabra

is this para

taxis

or is some sort of

logic

hidden

here

SATURNALIA

don't talk

big talk

me talk

leave message

date + time of call

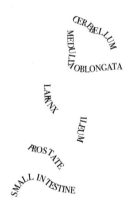

## 244

this sad tone
   is the move from voiced
to unvoiced plosive
    certain of the things i say
       i've sd before
   in another voice
to unvoice queue

## 245

I
am not
little corn

## 246

i being the pattern in the concrete
i being the droplet in the well
   pronouns whipping
  bodies into submission
personifiquantification

247

next time i see myself
gonna be
multicolored
man


248

Like Michaux said
world politics
doesn't matter much
if you've a pin in your eye—
unless your politics is
a pin in your eye


249

Because his father beat
him and his mother
he can't sleep at night
fans the flames of an insatiable ambition
writes constantly
is remembered as a
"great thinker"

250

*(commencement)*

the journalist imagines
   if you say
      "abandon tribalism"
            or
         "embrace tolerance"
   often enough
      people will start to do them
but all they learn from his advice
is to bark orders at each other


251

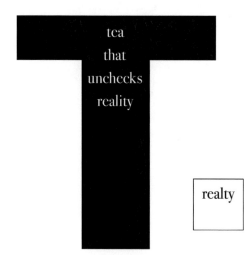

tea
that
unchecks
reality

realty

252

in the middle
   of this muggy spring
   a 60° night has us shivering
  the air is dry &
  has a different charge—
hint of another cold


253

   these didgits
   add up to ten
   again


254

in the middle of a drunken
argument i cdnt remember
what we were fighting about—
     feel like
     shit today

### 255

tea bag
into the basket from the bed
cat
between my feet
still can't shake it

### 256

pin wheel
ink well
framed on an axle
it depends
on the deep end
salinity
softshoe
spider

### 257

thief
thief
cant and cut
<invalid argument>
on either side
of the window

258

there's a cop in my backyard
with his foot on
a (crack)head
still
the bicycle's gone


259

Attention:
this poem
has been stolen


260

termite swarm
around the new backyard
floodlight
they seethe out of the ground
spontaneous
generation
millions of wings
white atoms
sphere of light

261

silly fears & lassitude
that turn the soul
like the stomach
upside down


262

thought i heard
something outside
but it's only
nanc breathing


263

sleep
these days
an ideal I
never quite attain


264

In the men's room at the bar
2 nights ago
a poem came to me
I thought to write it on my hand
but it was so great I knew
I wouldn't forget

265

phenomenology of fishing:
i cd lay here
and dream about it
all night


266

I don't mess around much
any more
there's nothing to mess around
to


267

Alex remarked
how the dog karoaked
when she walked


268

the best thing
about this book
is that i don't have to worry
like pound
about it being a botch

269

my ur-text
speaks all around


270

something in the rhythm
of the city
surge of bodies & words
that drains
the work
is the world


271

a dangerous trend
a downward spiral
a fascination with image


272

safety pin slide
speckled trout in the surf
not what brautigan
was after        periplum
language and dream
sunstroke
dehydration

### 273

*Words @ Work*

What would you do without em?
They're always on the job,
Whether hauling freight to Houston
Or waiting tables down on Rab.
From Africa to Alaska,
From Zlcen to Zanzibar,
From Boston to Yugoslavia,
From Wyoming to Clancy's bar.
They can handle the big stuff.
They can chop down a yew.
Sometimes just when you need 'em,
Words work– words work for you!


### 274

pit bull culture–
        snarl of race


### 275

more and more
the mental is the physical
despair is only fatigue
hope is no hangover

276

I'm working hard in bed
and way down
beside me
at the very
bottom
of a tall
glass
of water
is
the
emerald city


277

90% of writing
is learning to avoid
both perspiration
and inspiration


278

but if you don't live
w/ the fear stirring your insides
& you very well might not lots of people
don't lots of people I think
are happy
you have no reason to believe
anything

### 279

my domain is mean
like the streets
between the sheets


### 280

botox
inject mold
so you won't get old
(I'm cold)


### 281

from over the back fence
sound of violent retching
neighborhouse
going to crack
here we sleep
in the horror of
the street
eric & erica

### 282

Loss G.'s *Digital Poetics:*
Ong & the transition
oral to print to digital, hartman
   etc.— does the shift in media have
    one tenth the effect
  of the geometric increase
in sheer volume?


### 283

the way the poem goes
   through each of you
my mother doesn't belong
  in this crowd
I read these poems to her
   on her death-bed
the way the poem goes
   through each of you
the dead don't belong
  in this crowd


### 284

   author-ity— yes
the author is
  itty bitty

gods are just
    nouns showing off
a class in aesthetics
    is just folding up
    colorfully
    typographically
        into a box

*jihad*
        the crackdown on crack
*jihad*
        the tightening of the clamp
        the building blocks to the top
*jihad*
        corporate body, gathered for arrest power
*jihad*
        i'm a klutz when it comes to paper
        season of acquisition, on edge

### 287

the TV is male
the fridge is male
all the doors &
moldings are male—
but the odds are 50-50
for each individual
                    item


### 288

*parece que quiere llover*
  it seems it wants to rain
getting to the root of
  *tinte damas*


### 289

4:30 AM in another country
insomnia=jet lag in this language
    curtains painted on
movement
  trick of the eye

290

Europe as protracted
time lag:
pentagenarian
"voices" that keep us awake
5 geraniums


291

laughter echo
lalic like
the bottom of a pool
waking life
all around


292

fractaled/heliotropic
surface of the planet
serves sleep
to those deserving


293

the wrenched
are different
from ewe and eye

294

*for Vincent– Prague 7/6/02*


the place infects
    and then defects
turning insoluble
    just as identity might  enclose
and then embrace
    a way of being    now removed



295


    our mouth
    connexion
to each other & the mineral
    speaking like eating
      like kissing
not blurting but
gathering in



296


AAAAAAAAAA
IDENTITY
a n t h i l l
like an echo
body dissolved in

297

say the self is social
but if you've ever had
amoebae
multipying in your guts
you know how it is
to have certainty
shaken


298

call me paranoid
but I'm thinking terrorist


299

*Venezia 2002*

and if you think the gondolas
were expensive *that* year
reading 76 at the Miracoli
new nazi graffitti along
the giudecca canal
and at the festa del redentore
you cd have walked across
on the motorboats

300

a weird sort of paideuma—
German boats with Japanese motors
        on the ancient waters
    street musicians playing Chubby Checker
thought the boatsmanship was pure Venetian
    & the glass sellers having a horrible year
        due to the dollar's suddenly going flaccid
            against the fabulous EURO
because a Texas frat boy & bar-b-que buddies
            cooked up a way
    to sell everyone's future short


301

    jesse said
    she's going to bed
        to cuddle with
        a cuttlefish


302

    even airconditioning
    seems benevolent here
        & the TV makes a noise
        nanc thought was a rooster

at 2 AM
out the hotel window
across the courtyard
into the window
of the neighbor's house
I've sniffed out
   a screensaver

was thoreau
  a goody 2 shoes?
    civil disobedience OK but
anybody gets upset
  when you attack
    their sacred toes

la luna complete
  over brunnenburg
    elisabeta (one t) speaks English
      left the bill on my pillow
called me a taxi
  for 5 AM
    & the church bells
    rang @ 3

## 306

*27-07-02*

this morning Praga
this evening Fraga
Steven & Allen & Miroslav
      I can't reach you
even on my cellphone
     dobrou noc


## 308

The storks of alcala de henares:
1.  aren't in the guide books
2.  sound like roto-hammers
3.  glide over Cervantes'
    house like spindly
    knights or
    harpies out of
    hell

## 307

each contact
is a contract
body shrinks
pupils tighten
the idioma we receive
for the idioms we give
incorporated
in social product


## 309

yemas de avila—
  st. theresa's rosary
    and the finger that counted it
franco kept the hand by his bed
  his bride in a pun
    just the proximity of that power
that converted edith stein
  ("judea intelectula")
    @ auschwitz
(second) hand of christ's
  lover
    the arrow through the yolk

310

what the city wants
                    it takes
like oleander or banana
green feral parrots
that don't even
say hello


311

television replaces church
with rituals equally
arcane and complex
  like *big brother*


312

vltava rising
      just after we left
      the old haunts on TV
the prague zoo
a capsized ark
      gorilla drowning in his new apartment
      the old elephant up to his ears in sludge
          sea lions took off
          down the muddy river
we pray our friends
      are high and dry
      and for the zookeepers

313

poemwrittenwhilesleeping   crushe
                                    tee a
        what you mea
                    sev


314

in (the event of) somnia
    take 2 for
      word image replace
      image christ image
                    crushed


315

                a long tail
        of things slipping
            one by one
        like sheets
sleek now


316

    & just when you
        happen
        to think of it: it's ten again:
            <digit A.M.>

## 317

one morning Jimmy woke up
with the biggest hardon he'd
ever seen
it towered over him
big as a marlin
"Mom" he yelled

## 318

*the tilde over the past*

~

put presidents to pasture
put lime in the graves

## 319

n
a
r
r
a
t to have certainty shaken
one morning Jimmy woke up
v
e

o o
f v
p e
copyright law r
u e
the text u
s s
i i
deed to the city n
e i
n
g

320

that's all you need:
    a hayride


321
*for alex, 8-31-02*

nobody has time for
       semaphor
when you're drunk


322

& again
   frustration
on the business end


323

email from the poetuncle
ruins my night
that idiotic eloquence
makes me wanna just
    be quiet

324

a poetry that might
  continue
when the mind stops


325

gone over
      gone lover
go hover
in the nicht hut
      o lower mouth
  there's a frayed bit
of canvas back


326

the day
  is gray
& there's nothing to do
    oh joy
        oh boo hoo

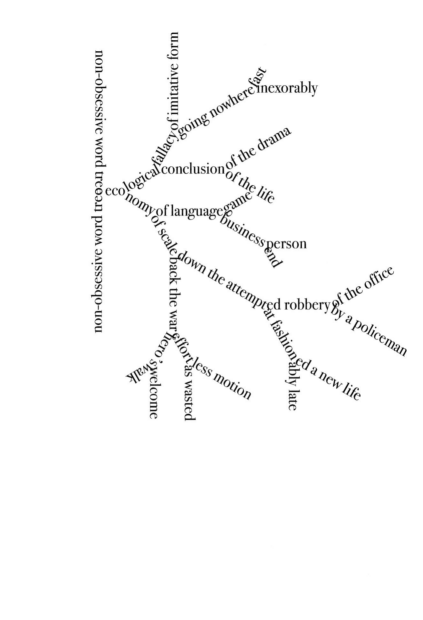

328

that one lying in bed
having his sleep ruined
by reenactments of work
concerns me less than myself
which drifts w/o anchor
above him
& below


329

what we know about each other

would fill a book about this size

dog barking / car pulling away


330

to get old
  to get old and have nothing
   to get old and have nothing
    and leave nothing
    behind
sweet nothing
sweet sweet
      nothing

331

that envelope on the floor
gives me an idea:
    gonna lay down in it
    and mail myself to you


332

what sounds dumb to you
  might be numb to you
    might be mum's the word
might be sounds like gum
or like a gun in a
'68 ford


333

confessed to *unemployment* believing in fairy tales
  to the crime of pederasty
confessional poetry bores even skunks
  performance a la nicolas roeg *hack* *genius* con
flagration of the holy *war* water
flagellation of the *mind your manners* body of water

334

once again, half a score
    every nine
till volume break the sequence
    numbers or
  what lumbers
along beside

335

space station  invention  poems sleeping women in iran  industry  jihad  history  bureaucracy  oil  drought  Foucault  angel

face of a tyrant
?

be an acter

concepts as activity
identity as activity

a picture
in captivity

337

What's it like to get old?
I used to look in mirrors.

338

the self object
of self subjected
injects defective
   germ    (secret: jacques lacan
         loves jennifer lopez)

*J.La*
*+*
*J.Lo*

339

   all there is
   that nothing
   take
   transcendeth
    time &
    gule

340

  liquidity
   vacuity
 benignity
 indignity  in the big
    city

341

Bush as futurist– like Marinetti
hurrying along the
'man becoming metal'
& the new digital
aesthetics
of war


342

or as skip sd.
9-11 was
first and foremost
art


343

maybe that's
what i mean
about not wanting
poetry to matter

344

that "quiet desperation"
that "most people" live (Thoreau)—
 part of the romantic vision is
 that the common herd be incapable

345

fan noise, numbing heat
even on 9-20-02—
isidore in the gulf—
we picked up our
new puppy
today

346

The dog was worrying game?

I want to be fireman when I grow up.

Is it all piece of rawhide bone.

There were 8 of us and a red VW bug on our tail.

pretending not to revise
is like
pretending to be asleep–
no one will ever know
and it doesn't matter
anyway

*for megan and dave, 9/22, 1:49 PM*

liminal time
inherit the planet
may the subway come to the surface
liminal
be secret joy

love, bill

### 349

After 30 hours with us
the new puppy has already sussed
the delicate spatial hieracrchies
maintained between Nanc & me & cat
knows when to bark & when
to hide behind us
musical connexion
as far above this grayed out america
sad sick america
as moon above earth.

### 350

it's nifty
to be thrifty
anyway who knows
one day you might
be sixty

### 351

gardenia
beside the bed
as isidore approaches
sweet scent
as maelstrom approaches

352

this dryness of the air
after the storm
reminds me of death—
the body politic
breathing the common
atmosphere


353

if there is (and there is)
    an end
to the chain of reasons
   then the reasons are themselves
without reason (and they are)


354

    gel roller retractable
w/ ergonomic grip
    one continuous line
   never skipping
for a thousand
    sheets
a thousand
miles

## 355

Lili you're my  
       a  
     second  
      l  
      i  
      s  
      t  
   hurricane  
       o  
  this month


## 356

        instant fame  
     automatic authority  
offshoots of no business  
       and  
  books that make  
     sense


## 357

New YorK:  
   the big big  
   of the small small:  
sleeping on the couch @  
     Polly and Andrew's  
pretending to be asleep  
     when they walk through

A:  I want to go down
        down into the town
B:  If you go down
        to the town you'll drown
A:  But why wd I drown
        I can swim in a town
B:  Because of the sound
        you'll drown in the sound

head
    down
to the
    cellar
to recuperate
    the stair
changes
    direction
7 times

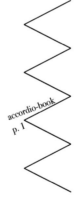

accordio-book
p. 1

360

is it possible to be a pessimist
  without taking a little sadistic
  pleasure in the pose?
or an optimist without owning
  a trace of moral superiority
    for holding out the hope?

Outside the university building
four boys take turns preaching.

*New Orleans, October 2001 – Octovber 2002*